PRAISE FOR
ROLE OF LOVE

"Paul has opened his soul and life experience in this book. His experiences give him a powerful insight into the power of love and how it can change anyone."

— **KADE JANES**, owner of Iron Gate Therapy

"His transformation, since beginning the Roll of Love, witnessed first hand. Having known Paul personally, for decades, I can attest to the following. He has become noticeably more kind. His increased graciousness radiates in his demeanor. Always a good listener, he listens ever more patiently, truly wanting to learn about and from others."

— **LOWELL REX**, Business Transformation Expert, Epic Business Coaches

"A new approach to business and personal growth without big dollar investments. See, and feel, the returns with a few minutes a day."

— **JEFF MATHER**, Small Business Owner/Business Counselor

"Paul Zolman's *The Role of Love* is a book that has the power to transform your life. You can read about the power of Love all day long, but until you actually practice Love, you won't really know what Love is. This book not only explains the different Love Styles, but it gives you a simple and easy way to thoughtfully practice Love in your daily life. And when you use the accompanying Love Dice, it's also fun! *The Role of Love* will open your mind and heart to a deep and abiding understanding of the true nature of Love. Everyone should read this book and DO this book."

— **MARGUERITE BONNETT**, Prolific Ghost Writer/Author

"Paul's vulnerable, warm, and wise narrative weaves together his personal (and often painful) quest to connect lovingly, his thoughtful insights about how love works in real life, and his generous offer of a genius gift, the Role of Love Game. Along with the inspiration and warm fuzzies of his story, he presents you with a tiny cube that promises to unlock your very own adventures in loving. Will you take the gamble, give it a spin, and watch those around you light up in brand new ways? Become a love linguist and watch the light - and love - ripple out!"

— **DEBI BARMONDE**, Inner Compass Life

Role of Love

PAUL ZOLMAN

Role of Love

THE MOST EFFECTIVE WAY TO DEMONSTRATE LOVE EVERY DAY

Copyright © 2023, Paul Zolman

ISBN Softcover: 979-8-9875243-0-5
ISBN Ebook: 979-8-9875243-1-2

All rights reserved. No part of this book may be reproduced or transmitted in any form or by any means, electronic or mechanical, including photocopying, recording, or by any information storage and retrieval system, without permission in writing from the copyright owner. For information on distribution rights, royalties, derivative works, or licensing opportunities on behalf of this content or work, please contact the publisher at the address below.

Printed in the United States of America.

Although the author and publisher have made every effort to ensure that the information and advice in this book were correct and accurate at press time, the author and publisher do not assume and hereby disclaim any liability to any party for any loss, damage, or disruption caused from acting upon the information in this book or by errors or omissions, whether such errors or omissions result from negligence, accident, or any other cause.

roleoflovedice.com

TABLE OF CONTENTS

Introduction 1

PART ONE 7
Chapter 1: The Role of Reality 9
Chapter 2: The Role of Authenticity 21
Chapter 3: The Role of Observation 29

PART TWO 39
Chapter 4: The Role of the Roll 41
Chapter 5: The Role of Words 47
Chapter 6: The Role of Service 55
Chapter 7: The Role of Touch 63
Chapter 8: The Role of Gifts 71
Chapter 9: The Role of Time 79

PART THREE 87
Chapter 10: The Role of Recognition 89
Chapter 11: The Role of "Light Me Up" 99

An Invitation 107
About the Author 109

This book is a tribute to those who will change their world by choosing to love consciously every day.

INTRODUCTION

For a very long time, I have seen great value in learning the art of investing. But the biggest thing I have found is that if you make a small investment and get great returns, you are going to try it over and over again until you have achieved the levels you want from that investment. Then, you may want to share the secret with others. Such is this book. I have found something that absolutely works and I am to the point of wanting to share. But it has nothing to do with money.

I invest two seconds of my time each day to set a theme or mantra for the day. You might think I live in Las Vegas when I tell you what I do. I roll a die. I know, it's not quite the same as throwing a dart for your personal financial investments. It's a die I created where each side has the roles of love in life. The Role of Love in anybody's life. The role of touch. The role of time. The role of words. The role of gifts. The role of service. The role of surprise when you find opportunities to love in a different genre than what you rolled for the day.

The Role of Love die works like this. You roll the die every day. Each day it will land on an icon of love. Whatever it lands on is the type of opportunities for loving you are watching for on that day. The next day it might be different, but over a thirty-day period, you will learn all the basic roles of love. It's a beautiful thing to understand the roles of love and learn how to give love away.

By doing this daily for several years, I have come to realize a few things about love. Number one, it's fruitless and frustrating to keep expectations of love coming your way because of something you have said or done. To clarify, that expectation of love returning in reciprocity, is totally something that I discovered was out of my control. I cannot bid love to come to me in a nice neat package that I might recognize as love.

Secondly, I only have control over the love I give away. To me, what I give away is love, but the recipient may not recognize it in that way. I do have control over whether I keep trying to discover the role of love they might enjoy best. As I try different roles of love, I might hit upon something that really lights them up. That's when I take a mental note, "Oh, that's what they like." From that mental note, I can try it again with greater precision. Not that I would read their face and suppose or assume what they like, but I would have valuable data to make better decisions on how to love that person.

The reaction of the person I am giving love to is also something I don't control. When I send love in one way, it may not be what they were expecting as love or kindness. For example, if you gave a person ice cream as a gift for a treat, they might not receive it as love because you didn't know they were lactose intolerant.

Adverse reactions that others might have to your expression of love should not deter you from your new mission to love all those you come in contact with in some way. This is the role of love. It is the ability to continue to love, without the expectation of recompense. It's loving because loving is the right thing to do. It's loving because you want to do your part to make the world a better place. It's loving because we have great historical examples that have given us the wisdom to do this and the results are well published. We want to follow those sterling examples. It's loving because that's the attitude that you prefer over being judgmental. It's loving because those thoughts of giving love away are the only way to maintain good thoughts about another person. This type of loving allows you to have beautiful thoughts of others constantly. There's great power in that firmness of mind to love. True love is constant and powerful. This is a perfection of your thoughts to get to that level. Part-time love or partiality of love doesn't qualify for true love at all. And the recipients feel it, genuine or not.

As the attitude of continually loving takes hold, you will be able to remember and store the information to be a better love purveyor in the future. Love is really all about observation and action based on that observation information. If the other person or audience lights up, you can feel more assured that you have found a role of love that resonates with them.

In the beginning, it may seem unnatural. I can give you that. It also may be awkward for you and others who knew your previous other personality. Rest assured, you are not giving up a personality that is good, but only replacing the personality, with love, that dims the light in another with love. Your new-found role is to brighten the days of those within your reach. My own personal guarantee is that if you heighten your awareness of love and your determination to love, that loving will soon and easily become natural to you in a very short period of time. This really is overnight wealth to all those who can apply the principles of this book.

Maybe one of the most gratifying experiences for me happened just a few months ago when I was visiting my new granddaughter. Many friends and neighbors were gathered to wish this new granddaughter good health and a good life. A celebration of a new birth. The help was astounding! I found the people who were responsible for the great feast and celebration. I thanked them and expressed my gratitude to them. Their response was, "I feel validated." No one has ever responded to me like that in my life. I felt validated for remembering to be grateful.

So when do we love? When it's convenient? When the opportunity presents itself? When we think about it? Willie Nilly? Surely there's a better way.

I found this die very helpful to focus on loving constantly. The discovery is that what you focus on becomes larger in your life. If you focus on another's problems, then the problems are magnified. The focus on your own problems makes them bigger than life. When you are looking for what is good about another person, you also have the opportunity to size that quality up for that person. We all have faults. We all make mistakes. But to consciously choose to recognize the good that people do is the remedy for crowding out the evil of the day. Don't give utterance or attention to evil but rather accentuate the good.

Concentrating my focus on love also helped me discover that I had zero time for judgment. Judgment was 180 degrees from my new line of sight. Judgment didn't have a role in my new eyes as it verbalized the excellent qualities of others. It was crowded out. For me, that was a new phenomenon. I seriously found that my two-second investment was paying dividends that I could have never imagined! Life without having to judge others? Do you mean I don't have to gossip? I don't have to try to figure out why that neighbor parked in front of my house? I love this new life!

Interest in people and who they are and what they do continues to amaze me. I have found myself talking to perfect strangers trying to find out something good about them. The quest is for something they have discovered as their success in life. It's amazing how real conversations actually have allowed me to make connections to their life I only thought Facebook able to do electronically. At church on Sunday, a new family was introduced as having moved into the neighborhood. They moved from Missouri but knew my wife's brother and nephew. This was only discovered by asking non-threatening questions which encouraged them to freely tell their story. We made the connection!

However, for me, it wasn't always this way. I had to overcome darkness to find this light and the Role of Love in my life.

Part One

Chapter 1

THE ROLE OF REALITY

"No one is born hating another person because of the color of his skin, or his background, or his religion. People must learn to hate, and if they can learn to hate, they can be taught to love, for love comes more naturally to the human heart than its opposite."

— NELSON MANDELA —

You would think I was a hardened criminal the way my attorney, the prosecuting attorney, and the judge looked at me. It was the type of look that muttered, "I'm going to nail you to the wall." No, I had never received that look before, but I had possibly projected it out there for it's not-so-serendipitous return. Why now? I slapped my three-year-old son for knocking off my wife's glasses while reading the Bible. That's the most complicated sentence you will read in this text.

I was raised by a father who drove semi-trucks and was gone most of the week. He would usually return on Friday for his date with my mother. He never missed. I loved that example then and I love it now. However, the venue and what happened on that date was fairly predictable. Always the Maverick Bar. Always drinking. My mother would somehow disgorge what had happened that week, good and mostly bad. From that, we would either get the belt, spankings, or a chance to spend time with him, also at the Maverick Bar. Of the good times at the Maverick Bar as a child, I remember that I totally disliked the contaminated 7-up drinks, but enjoyed shooting pool at the pool table. This was a date??

Depending upon the severity of the infractions of the week, my reward would apparently be just, in my father's eyes. Maybe he thought he was milder than his own father who died when he was just ten years old. There must have been times that I was absolutely horrible! I say that because I remember being black and blue on my rear for more than three weeks after one session. After another, I decided to take my life. But, all I had was a pocket knife with a one inch blade. I pressed the tip to my chest where I thought my heart was and it hurt a bit. That got me thinking. This one-inch blade isn't going to do anything to me but hurt me and definitely not kill me. After I hurt myself, then my mother is going to tell my Dad and I am really going to get hurt then. I stopped the process and cried myself to sleep.

I loved my father and wanted to grow up to be just like him, smoking Viceroy cigarettes and everything. My mother's Winston cigarettes seemed wimpy to me compared to Viceroy. I would even compare notes with my friends as to what they were going to smoke when they got older. Lots of Marlboro men in the making during the day. We always played the "my dad is better than your dad" game. Except he wasn't. All along, my parents told me not to smoke or drink, while they blew smoke rings into the air.

By age seventeen, the disconnect between my parents' words and actions became so annoying that I became quite the contrarian. Anything my father wanted to do, I did not want to do. We couldn't connect on any subject except that he baked

CHAPTER 1: THE ROLE OF REALITY

great chicken every Sunday and that he purposefully dated my mother.

Before I ever got married, I committed to myself that I would not be rough or even close to being as rough as my father was with us. Those things about my father I absolutely did not want to replicate and transfer to my children. Back then, I didn't know about generational cycles of abuse and how your childhood trauma can affect your behaviors as an adult.

I was actually a good kid. I was a boy between two girls, so I thought I was pretty mild since my closest friends were girls and happened to be my sisters. The judge didn't agree that I was mild. Just five months earlier, I reported myself for hitting my son for intervening between a verbal disciplining of one of his siblings. I was so very sorry for what I had done that I reported the incident to the police. The child was examined and I was warned. I had been warned. When I slapped the three-year-old, I also felt horrible and reported myself to family services. They weren't answering the phone, so I left a message on my way to work, pleading for help with my problem. This was the evidence that was going to nail me to the wall. The Family Services response was in the form of a visit to my home, where my wife was with the younger children.

They also quickly visited the school and pulled the other children out of class to interview them. I was called later that day by my wife stating that I was forbidden to even come near our home by the agency and now the police were involved. I returned from work that night to stay with a friend and talk to the police chief. After trying to defend my discipline of the three-year-old, I was given my rights while the chief and I rode in the squad car around town. No escape. I was booked on charges of child abuse and was fingerprinted. My call to them was for help, maybe a counselor or some classes. So far, I wasn't getting any help.

My plea in court was guilty. After all, I had reported myself and I did slap the child. I didn't see the need for a prolonged court process, nor for dragging the rest of the family into court to testify against their father. I had done it and knew I had done it. I wanted to stop the behavior of any kind of abuse and become a loving father, somehow, someway. The judge sentenced me to a yearlong course of anger management and eighteen months' probation for slapping my child. No bruises, no broken bones, no marks. That was my help. Punishment instead of education. It's really too bad that there isn't any help between the problem and sentencing. I needed interim help and knew I needed the help and wanted it. I wanted to break the cycles of abuse that were common in my parents' generation. I was in hot water. I wanted to change my thought processes rather than serve a sentence that may or may not rehabilitate me.

I've heard that cold water is better if you want to change your thoughts. But ok, let's see how this shakes out. I felt I was already getting better by not getting mad about having to drive the eighty-mile round trip for the course and pay $25 per class. I could not miss or I would get a jail sentence. $1400 for the year and it had to be in cash. No vacations or traveling out of state that year. My mother must have felt some culpability for the anger as I remember her sending me a check for $1400 to cover the cost of the class. Or was it out of love? I was so confused.

The class was not about anger so much as it was about trying to reform aggressive violence in the community. Good idea, right? One classmate told a story about how he had held his wife up by the neck, against the wall, feet off the ground, until she fainted. Another had whipped his girlfriend so bad she was in the hospital. We received a book that was spiral bound and we were expected to write in the book our feelings about each discussion. The written homework was reviewed and apparently used as evidence against some of my fellow classmates. If I was angry, then these guys attending and giving the class were crazy. The instructors seemed to use various means to bring out stories of other acts of violence to pile onto the current charges, create new charges, or solve a cold case. This was the teaching environment for learning how not to get so angry.

My biggest remembrance of the class was a pinwheel of abuse. It had thirteen types of abuse and descriptions of how they might manifest. Pet abuse, economic abuse, verbal, physical, and emotional abuse were among the flavors of abuse I saw on the wheel. It could almost be called the wheel of misfortune. As I reviewed this wheel of misfortune, I began to feel guilt, but I didn't really understand how to make the attitudes go away. Then I had a thought… what if I found out the opposite of the specific abuse? And if I focused on those opposites, would that give me new attitudes and a new heart and something to really work on? It was a private realization and even then, I didn't know if it would work.

As it was, I was guilty of maybe half of the abuses listed on the wheel. I had seen them or participated in them. This was an eye-opener to me. So much damage had been done and I didn't know how to remove the pain I had caused. Eventually, it ended my marriage of twenty-three years and eight children. My wife was looking elsewhere for love. Even though I may have caused the problem, she wasn't allowed in my book to go find other men. Well, she did and we ended that marriage relationship. I had to make better choices.

Anger seems to be more of a knee-jerk reaction than a choice. But it also seemed like a choice not to find a substitute for the thoughts leading up to the reaction. How was I going to make the change? In reviewing the opposites on the wheel, I realized that, in every case, love could have been the answer rather than abuse. I knew I needed to either look for love or learn more about it and make a determination to practice love no matter what. I needed to distance myself from the events that put me in hot water.

I soon realized that love is also a choice. It's a two-way street. I came to realize that we only have the power to give love away. What comes back to us is really not our choice. Nor would we want it to be our choice. Controlling or manipulating what comes back is exactly that; control and manipulation. Our reaction to what comes back is our choice. Love given freely, seems to be love truly given from the heart. Love that is extracted or forced is less than the feeling of love. It's something else. My journey has given me insight and knowledge about trying to make love happen.

Just like the song, I was guilty of looking for love in all the wrong places. It's kind of a catchy line of lyrics, but is there meaning behind it? Let's break it down a little. Why is anyone out there looking for love in the first place? Is love such a 'thing' that can be tangible enough to be looking for it? Or Heaven forbid, buy it?

After some rough patches in my own life, I have to admit I didn't want to even think about love. I created my own mid-life crisis instead. My idea was to have fun. And I am sure, in the back of my mind, I thought I might meet someone in the process. Well, I was half right. I did have a lot of fun doing what I called 'destination dating.' I would find a looker online, do the normal interview questions based upon my criteria, and set the date in a spot neutral to both parties. It was at this destination where the date happened.

Part of the criteria was that they needed to have some spiritual depth. To ascertain this online was quite the trick. To parse truth from the fluff of the person I was considering, I would ask questions that would require some spiritual background to know. Did they read the scriptures? What was their favorite bible story? Did they rely on and believe in prayer? Tell me about an answer to your prayers. Of course, the normal things would come up about their ex. How they described their ex and the current relationship with their ex also factored into whether an invitation would be extended for a date. As the date approached, what to do was a great discussion. How they made those little decisions was something I was observing as well. Children from their previous marriage and the arrangements was more of an information question, not really a criterion for dating or not. I LOVE children and the more the merrier to me.

Talking to women has always been easier for me than talking to men. I was number ten of eleven children and was born with an older sister right above me and a younger sister right below. My parents said I was the baloney between two slices of white bread. And then they would laugh. I didn't get their joke for a long time. Verbal abuse wasn't funny. I played with these sisters growing up and was commanded to be nice to them or suffer the wrath of my father. He really respected women and doted quite heavily on my sisters. In that circumstance, I also grew up not wanting to get grease under my fingernails, unlike my father the mechanic or my brothers that followed in his footsteps.

All this destination dating was fun, but short-lived and it produced zero lasting relationships. In eighteen months, I had been to Atlanta, Jacksonville, New York City, Cabo San Lucas, Phoenix, Salt Lake City, Kansas City, Nashville, Charlotte, Columbia, and Charleston, South Carolina, and many other places. The online interview questions were helpful to get back into the dating game. After all, I had been married over twenty-three years and it was definitely awkward at first.

The thought occurred to me as to why I was looking for love. Why did I want to be loved? And truly, is love something to find? All the travel for these dates produced a paradigm shift for me. I thought, instead of looking for love far away, what would happen if I decided to just GIVE love away right where I was? What would happen if I was the giver of love rather than the frustrated one trying to find someone to love me?

I started sincerely trying to learn the names of my neighbors, bank tellers, store clerks, people at church, sports buddies, gas station attendants, etc. With the electronic age of phones and online distancing, many were a little spooked when I treated them like a person. Conversations, no matter how small, became a surprise to some of them. It didn't matter to me if they remembered my name or not. I listened. I watched. I observed. So much information comes in through conversation and body language. Soon, I took them treats. Not long after that, dinners and parties followed. I truly became more aware of my surroundings, right near my home. I volunteered for a non-profit helping kids be able to have lunches over the weekend and then designed a visitor guide for a local Chamber of Commerce. When I gave time, effort, and love to the neighborhood and community, guess what happened? Love came to me unabated. No longer did I have to look or search or find or seek… Love came to me.

My discovery in all this was that love is a privileged society. Those who give it, get more and give more. It's interesting to me how giving increases your capacity to give. It is kind of like exercising a muscle and seeing that muscle grow stronger. I determined that each day I would exercise my love muscles and give to all that I came in contact with. It was definitely a different tact from just loving those close to me and forgetting about others. A line from the Count of Monte Cristo verifies this thought: "Love is for those who give it."

Those who live within the rules of this country club of love give it freely without a need or desire for accolades or fanfare. It is to these selfless stalwarts of the community that we all gravitate and desire to be more like. They serve, they plant seeds of goodness, they speak kind words, and they may think you are the only one in the world when it comes to spending time. You know them in your community. You love and admire them in your community. The cleverer ones remain anonymous for their own reasons but mostly to have more time to spend doing what they love... giving love.

In this period of change, I have discovered that the best giving of love happened when I was doing it without pomp and circumstance. I wanted to follow in the footsteps of these giving people of the community. I began quietly feeding the homeless, ringing doorbells, leaving treats, and running like crazy as not to be caught doing good. There was no bugle and fife, neither drum nor banner. Not a single toot of my own horn would interrupt the peace I felt as love came to me. All the pity parties ceased. The pity parties were when I waited for things to happen while I was doing nothing. The pity parties stopped when I stopped looking for love and started giving love to all those with whom I came in contact. I learned how to give love in all the styles of love and enjoyed the challenge of trying to be creative when doing so.

Someone has wisely said, 'Lift where you stand.' I would suggest that we love where we live. It is the right place and it is the most critical time to do so. Enough with hate. Enough with looking for love in all the wrong places. Love where you live and watch your community transform. It only takes a little bit of goodness to lift the spirits of everyone. Have you done any good in the world today? Try it. It makes you feel great!

Chapter 2

THE ROLE OF AUTHENTICITY

> *"People will forget what you said, people will forget what you did, but people will never forget how you made them feel."*
>
> — MAYA ANGELOU —

I was seventeen years old when it occurred to me that sometimes words and actions don't match. MY words and actions. Days of realizations can be good in the long run, but the short run stinks. Such was that time. I remember being mad at myself when I caught myself having inner and outer conflict, yet again. I still get upset about it, but not as much as then. E.F. Hutton, an investment brokerage at the time, had a tagline that I remember: "When E.F. Hutton speaks, people listen." I wanted that parity of words for myself. When I said something, I wanted people to know that I was being genuine and authentic.

It was this time of my life that I began to be interested in accounting and business in general. I moved from my home in Montana after my junior year of high school to be in a better environment where I could start matching my words and actions better. Running away from circumstances was my plan for change. My journey took me to my older brother's home in California and I found a job as a bookkeeper with the company he worked for. It bugged me that in business you bought something and then you told the customer a different price. In this self-righteous crusade of having words and actions match, I didn't know if I could ever be in business. The whole idea that you bought something for one price and told someone else it was another price and sold it to them was distorting the circle of integrity that I had drawn. Ughhhh! Would I ever understand this complex world?? Was being authentic that subjective?

My niece was coming to visit my brother one day and had her two-year-old son Phinn with her. When they were close, she quietly whispered to Phinn, "Phinn, I need you to look Uncle Paul in the eyes and say, 'Hi Paul.'" He did as he was so carefully and lovingly instructed by his mother. Looking into the eyes of a person is one of those characteristics of being authentic. I felt Phinn really made the effort to care about who he was talking with by eye contact. It didn't seem like a casual greeting in passing, like "how's it going?" It was direct and specifically for me. Peering into eyes, the windows of a soul, can really help you be authentic in your words and actions. Some express this kindness of authenticity with the soft tone of voice. Others put their arm around you and whisper into your ear sweet somethings. They really are somethings because the soft tones and kind words whispered will stay with the receiver for a long time. I love these moments. They warm my heart and maybe yours as well.

My wife expresses gratitude to those who speak in church. She sends notes to those who do a kindness that maybe they thought no one noticed. Many recipients of these notes have come up to her and said it was the first personal note they have gotten through snail mail in a VERY long time. Or, they express how they genuinely felt the kindness. It's a simple thing that brings great returns for the investment of time and energy.

CHAPTER 2: THE ROLE OF AUTHENTICITY

Gratitude is one of those attributes that contribute to being authentic. You probably wouldn't express gratitude to an opponent for missing a shot, having a double fault, or other mistakes they may have made. That's more like sarcastic humor. Gratitude seems to be attention to the genuinely good things that people do and accomplish. Gratitude will also open doors of kindness to the giver of the kindness. Kindness begets kindness. Gratitude begets gratitude. Authenticity begets authenticity.

As we study this subject of authenticity, we may want to do an inventory of our own vocabulary. How many words do we say that actually mean something else? Sick. Wicked. Incredible, just to name a few. Sick used to mean something that was not well. Now it could easily mean something that is amazing. Wicked used to mean something that was from the Devil. Now it also has an opposite meaning of being something sweet, rather than bitter. Incredible is a word that means not credible, but usage is more of something that is spectacular or amazing. See the disparity? Can you see my struggle?

This was the family I grew up in. Complicated. Difficult to express real feelings. And the misunderstanding that resulted was dysfunctional at best and elevated to anger or violence at worst. It took me a long time of studying vocabulary to find a GOOD vocabulary that would express how I really felt. It's not necessary to demean anyone for a fault or weakness. Use your words to lift and compliment and brighten and redeem. The attitude of Gratitude will build bridges, not burn them. It will extend the olive leaf to those who need it at the very moment they are in need. You can be their angel of mercy and cut them some slack. If you are doing this reconciliation inside, you will begin to realize that you also will have need of mercy for your foibles and fallacies when they are exposed. Certainly that day will come. Plan for it by giving mercy today and tomorrow and next week. How you treat others with mercy today may foreshadow how you might be treated for your own failings. Be kind and thoughtful with your words. Be genuinely kind with what you say.

When mistakes are made, which is inevitable, remember to apologize. Ask for the mercy and kindness and forgiveness of the person that may have chosen to be offended by your words or actions. This back and forth has a polishing effect. Think of this as waxing your car. You don't just set the polish in one place and hope that it will be buffed out. It's the back and forth or circular action that gives the gleam and smiles to the relationship. If someone rubs you the wrong way, how will you ever get polished? No relationship is perfect because people are not perfect. No comment is the best action and stinging reprimand for negative commentary. Leave the room and encourage their good behavior. Hold your tongue except for encouragement of good.

There was a time in my life that communication with my parents was required by the set of rules I chose to obey. I was called of God as a missionary to serve in Japan. I was required to write to my parents once a week for a period of two years. That was one rule of the monk-type setting I chose to become a part. After the two-year period, I mused to myself that writing them was a good habit. Since I was no longer 'required' to write them, I asked myself if I would throw away a good habit and abandon all I had learned in two years? I decided then and there that when I acquire a good habit, it's best to keep that habit. For 32 years, with only a few gaps, I wrote to my parents and subsequently just my mother after my father died, every week. Over 1500 letters. She used to tell me what day my letter would arrive. It was obvious that she waited and anticipated the letter on Thursday each week. I know she worried when she didn't get it.

Over time, I realized that it was a great time to thank my parents for all they had done for me. It was also a great time for honoring them. It was a great time to share my life and my doings with them. As parents, they still wanted to be part of my life and be happy with my successes and supportive in my failures. My thoughts and stories were a way for them to relive their own parenthood, good or bad. I felt in those years I had a better relationship through correspondence than I ever did being with them in person. Yes, the fifth of the Ten Commandments is to honor our father and mother with the promise that our days would be longer. It puzzled me how I could be obedient to that particular commandment prior to my extended letter writing. I am so grateful I made the effort to keep the good habit I acquired. Gratitude for them was definitely a blessing for the twenty to thirty minutes per week it took to do this.

Again, I was back to my words matching my actions. Congruity and consistency at doing those things that really matter in life. Consistently. Habitually. Lovingly. Genuinely loving them and putting that love into words. Loving them gave me more love from them. They never hated me more for being kind to them. They even seemed to judge me less for my own weaknesses. The mercy was there. The kindness and interest was alive. The relationship was becoming stronger because of regular acts of kindness. It was highly recommended at the onset, but it seems so much more profound now that both my mother and father are gone. No regrets. No thoughts of wishing I was less kind or spent less time writing letters. This genuineness is something that can be done without regrets.

Authenticity becomes an asset as you practice it. It becomes a part of you that you have chosen. It becomes a character trait that you test and try and build and grow. If there is any way you want to be remembered after you are gone, authenticity is one of those traits you may want listed in your obituary.

Chapter 3

THE ROLE OF OBSERVATION

"If you are looking for a friend who is faultless, you will be friendless."

— RUMI —

In August of 2020, I was fishing on a lake near my home in Utah. My day started with me fishing near a few others and I had caught my first fish when another gentleman approached and ASKED if he could fish between me and the tree that was to my right on the shore. No one ever asks. I told him it was no problem. Soon, he had a fish on his line and the first thing I noticed was that he kept the tip of his pole pointed down into the water. Fishermen naturally watch each other to borrow ideas and try to get more fish. It seemed to me that doing this created less fight in the fish and less likelihood that the fish would get away. He gently reeled in the fish. Then, he did a curious thing. He left his pole on the beach and waded out into the water where the fish was at the end of his line. He lifted the fish ever so gently in the water and carefully removed the hook. Then, he let the fish swim away. There wasn't any trauma of the fish ever being out of the water. This man had his family with him and they were playing around while he fished. Their energetic exploration of the shore didn't deter the fish from taking the bait.

The next day, I decided to get up early, before the sun and head back up to this same spot. I was one of the first to arrive and maybe the first to get a line in the water. After about thirty minutes, this same gentleman came and again asked for permission to fish beside me, in the same spot as the previous day. He introduced himself as Joshua and that he worked in the Treasury Department for a local church. He was working remotely because of Covid 19. His grandparents had acquired a cabin on the lake in the 50's where he and his family were staying.

Somehow in the course of our conversation, he said that it was doing the little things in life that mattered and made great things happen. I told him that was my mantra for life and proceeded to tell him a bit about the choices I try to make each day to love. I created a die with styles of love on it. I told him about the die I roll every day so I can practice that style of love all day that day. He was amazingly intrigued and confessed he was a bishop of his home ward in Layton and that he could see a great need for a product like this. When he mentioned that he was a bishop, the name of a young saint came to mind, probably because of the youth of this man. Thomas S. Monson. I am guessing Joshua was in his late 20's or early 30's.

We were two religious men on the banks of the lake, fishing and telling stories. I was so very impressed with his unassuming attitude to request permission to fish beside me. I was equally impressed with his kindness to the fish that he caught. He went out to where they were... in the water and released many of them. There were overtones of other great men of history that have also gone to where 'fish' were and provided comfort or a release from pain. The light and love that I felt that day still touches my heart today.

CHAPTER 3: THE ROLE OF OBSERVATION

In this circumstance, I was already in the mode of watching for opportunities to love. It never crossed my mind in this journey of mine that I might see the virtues of love practiced in such a profound way... even to the fish. True love seems to have that constancy about it. It's an expression of love in everything we do. Therein seems to lie authenticity and sincerity, expressed by others. The courtesy practiced by Joshua to ask to fish beside me, seemed to be thoughtful and kind. It was unassuming. These new discoveries of qualities and traits of love have helped me better understand love. Constancy, authenticity, sincerity, courtesy, thoughtfulness, kindness, unassuming all seemed to have floated to the surface as I was watching for traits of love, as practiced by others.

Part of love seems for me to have morphed into watching for the virtues of others and expressing that with words or actions. The thought almost seems radical. Watch for the virtues in others? What if we only talked about those virtues? Everyone has faults, frailties, makes mistakes or has a handicap. Instead of comparing our handicaps to others, what would happen if we all noticed the virtues? What if we all talked about the virtues of others rather than their missteps and failings? What if we only talked about the superpowers of each other rather than the super weaknesses? If virtues were in our thoughts constantly, would we repel people or would they want to be near us? Sorry old people, no more medical ailment stories. Tell us what is good about you... and season that with what is right about you.

On one occasion a few years ago, I observed one of my nephews supervising his sister on one of her first times making pancakes. The first one didn't turn out so well. My nephew said to her, "It's all right. Maybe the next one will turn out better."

His voice was soft, yet very encouraging. She was determined to do better because of his kind words of validation.

World War 1 was from 1914 to 1918. War is not kind. There's a scripture that I remember because its reference reminds me of World War I if you don't do what it says to do. World War I was active in 1918 and so was the Spanish Flu Epidemic. The book of Leviticus in the Old Testament, chapter 19:18 says, "Thou shalt not avenge, nor bear any grudge against the children of thy people, but thou shalt love thy neighbor as thyself: I am the Lord." Certainly, if feelings of revenge or bearing a grudge against another is something you choose to do, it can escalate as you tell others and become a war eventually, if left to its own devices to grow and fester. Kill the weeds of those thoughts! There are better choices than to hold a grudge.

We can make this choice to love ourselves and love our neighbors equally. There's a song from the mid 1940's called Accentuate the Positive that tells us what to do with our words. In situations like Jonah in the whale or Noah in the Ark, where all seemed dark, they definitely looked at the positive. Each of us has dark moments and each of us has moments of brilliant light. In the dark moments, I have discovered that taking a pause to wait for the light is the best thing to do. Making any kind of major decision in the dark is setting yourself up for more darkness. Wait for the light, as painful as it might be. The sun will come up again tomorrow. Walk toward the light.

Darkness and light are in constant contrast. In the past several years it has been useful to me to discover the opposite of a thing to understand the meaning of a word, action or phrase. 'What is it not?' becomes the test. The breadth of a spectrum seems to be illuminated by visiting both sides of the issue.

CHAPTER 3: THE ROLE OF OBSERVATION

Let's talk about brotherly love as an example. It seems fairly difficult to define, so first let's talk about what it is not. It definitely is not being fleeting, unstable, fickle, selfish, possessive, jealous, or envious. Those seem more like the qualities of romantic love, and unless that romantic love is fortified by other kinds of love, it may not survive. Consider the current divorce rate and then revisit the words fleeting, unstable, fickle, selfish, possessive, jealous, or envious. Brotherly love also does not necessarily have the qualities of friendship although it may be a part of it. Friends like each other, delight in each other's companionship, are confidential, loyal, trusting, and share many mutual interests. Friendship is reciprocal.

True brotherly love is more unselfish than either romantic love or friendship. The apostle Paul said that Christian love "envieth not and seeketh not her own." One possessed of Christian love has a profound concern for the welfare of others. He loses his life in their interest. It doesn't matter whether the other person—the one loved—appreciates or responds to the love shown to him, because brotherly love nourishes itself. It resides wholly in the person who LOVES and doesn't need a response to keep it alive as romantic love and friendship do. I heard someone say the other day that friends stab you in the front and others stab you in the back. Brotherly love does neither.

Brotherly love, unlike romantic love or friendship, is impartial and, therefore, universal. One who has brotherly love is concerned for any and every man, whether he be sinner or saint, attractive or unattractive, of the same or of another faith or race. In fact, if one is selective as to whom he loves, the chances are he lacks love for all men in a brotherly way.

Brotherly love is essentially feeling an emotion, as are all kinds of love. However, it also has an intellectual component.

It takes reflection and self-discipline to desire, seek, be watchful, and identify the good of one who is antagonistic or repulsive. If you are watching for the good of others constantly, it seems that you are doing what I recognize as virtue garnishing your thoughts. All. The. Time. When you are constantly looking for the good in others and treating them with respect and admiration for that good, it crowds out any feelings you might have of any faults they might possess.

Magnifying glasses have always intrigued me. It's amazing how things get much bigger as we focus on them. The behaviors we focus on in others will grow and be magnified, too. Please choose well what you magnify. Choose the better part. Choose to magnify what's right about others instead of what might be perceived as wrong. Magnify the virtues of others. Maybe you remember Donny and Marie Osmond singing "Puppy Love…" It was describing the temporary love and cuteness of love in the beginning of a relationship. I don't recall them doing a sequel about the dog love that grew up out of that puppy love. It's more like "*Who let the dogs out*" by Baha Men. Ark, ark, ark, wan, wan, wan…

Brotherly love does not strike one spontaneously as romantic love might do. For this reason, it is the most stable and enduring of all forms of love. People err in thinking that because they love someone, they must always do their bidding. Some parents are afraid to say no or to be firm. People, especially youth, give in to friends, colleagues or associates against their better judgment for fear of offending, or of not being loving. Brotherly love is consistent with justice, with firmness, even with rebuke when the person is acting in the interest of others.

Brotherly love means, in the language of the philosopher Kant, to treat persons as ends, never as means to our own selfish ends. This means that in business, in dating, in marriage, at school, and at work, we don't use and abuse people as functions. Nor are they being purely instrumental to our own goals, but we treat them as whole persons and in their interest—we practice the Golden Rule. "Love thy neighbor" remains a fundamental law of peaceable human existence.

Part of this brotherly love consists of compassion. Dr. Kristin Neff, a psychologist studying self-compassion, has stated, "Compassion is, by definition, relational. Compassion literally means 'to suffer with,' which implies a basic mutuality in the experience of suffering." Thus, compassion is more than a recognition of an individual's negative experience and feeling badly about it. It implies an ability to "suffer with" an individual who is struggling. Some of you may have desires to suffer like Bill Gates or Jeff Bezos, with all their money and the problems they have. You might muse, I think I could suffer like that. This is not the suffering I am speaking about.

Empathy is a synonym of Compassion. Compassion and empathy require real work. It can be difficult to understand oneself or another person. It is even more difficult to enter suffering with oneself or another. Perhaps this difficulty is one of the things that leads us to the other side of the road, wanting to help but struggling to find the ability to enter suffering with self or with another. Yet a willingness to enter and understand suffering can be one of the most healing things we can do.

If we all learned to positively speak kind words to each other, to the animals, to fish, or whatever when we talk, we would develop that consistency of kindness called true brotherly love. How does your garden grow? Consider the virtues of others, express the goodness, magnify goodness and virtues and both the giver and receiver of love will be happy.

Chapter 4

THE ROLE OF THE ROLL

> "The day the power of love overrules the love of power, the world will know peace."
>
> — GANDHI —

I created the die as a tool to help me internalize the rules of love. Initially, I wanted to learn about the ways people send and receive love. Love seemed lacking in my childhood and I don't feel particularly unique to that circumstance. The principles I learned as a child were mostly of anger and control while the principles of love embody kindness and empowerment. It's a diabolical difference and what I would describe as a hole in my early childhood development.

The die creation for me was also a commitment to my decision to learn to love. Reading books is one thing, but if the books don't change your habits, what good are the books? I thought, what if I made learning to love a game? In my childhood, our family did play games. Usually, they ended in anger because someone bent the rules to their own benefit. However, when the rules were bent to my benefit, I didn't complain. I liked games when I could win. I thought I could win at the game of love. I had a lot to learn.

Growing up, love appeared fickle. It depended upon the day, the mood, the weather, the money in the bank (or lack thereof), bills paid or piled up. There were always conditions that made love seem like a fair-weather friend. Can you understand my dilemma?

We all have pivotal points in our life and education. Mine happened during my junior year of high school. I had a full-time job, went to school full-time, moved away from home, and bought my first car. Lots of changes and lots of growth. I had a moment of quiet contemplation that got me thinking about what is true… all the time. Not just true for today or for the moment, but all the time. What was consistent that was definitely out of my control?

One of the things I came up with was that the sun came up every day, regardless of anything I had done. It was faithful in that regard and so very constant and consistent. I also believed, and still believe, in a higher power I call God. There is a higher power that created the universe and makes the sun come up every morning. I couldn't have done that. How could I create a hill or mountain or water or streams or an eco-system? No, someone of a higher intelligence and power did that for what I believe to be a benefit to me. Because of my belief system then and now, I saw that this person loved constantly, consistently, and without fail. In my youth, I was just beginning to feel and understand that true love had qualities of constancy and steadiness.

The love of God was there regardless of what I did, just like the sun coming up. In fact, I believe that the sun coming up is one of those acts of love from that higher being. It's for our benefit. Love is for our benefit. The very fact that God gives and gives and gives without regard of persons is something for all to look at and consider the kindnesses granted to us daily. Shouldn't we be doing similar acts?

It's possible that love of someone close to you is being taken for granted. I found that rolling the die gives me eyes to watch for opportunities to love, as well as count the blessings of love coming my way from God, family, friends, acquaintances, and others. The eyes to see only came from practicing on a consistent basis the giving of love. With the giving came recognition. With the recognition came understanding. With the understanding came eyes that watched as others would love on me. It wasn't long before I could recognize the love and respond appropriately. With gratitude. Gratitude was definitely missing when I couldn't see the love someone was giving. Rolling every day gave me consistency in watching for opportunities, appropriately loving, and reacting lovingly to those who loved me.

The die consists of five basic styles of love and the roles they play in our life and the lives of others. Touch, Gifts, Time, Service, and Words. The sixth side of the die has a hand with a question mark in the center of the palm. This side is what I call Surprise me. The Surprise Me side of the die is the day you watch for any way to love others through your own observation. It can be as simple as a smile or as complex as helping someone find a job. It could be words, spending time, a hug, help, or a gift of one kind or another. Just two instructions: 1. Roll the die every day. 2. Practice that love style all day that day, to everyone in your reach.

The simplicity of the die is purposeful. I have always enjoyed doing a little to get a great reward. Small steps lead to great things. The journey of a thousand miles starts with the first step. It takes less than a couple of seconds to roll the die. The picture or icon on the die is there to help us remember throughout the day what we rolled. Pictures do that for us. The visual is much better for most people than a printed reminder that might not even be viewed. The picture can be recalled to the mind instantly. That's the power of the die.

Developing a habit of rolling the die daily and then extending that habit of doing the role of love will change your life. It has changed mine and I can guarantee your focus will change as well.

Fickleness in the love category will be gone. Consistently rolling, consistently doing, consistently becoming someone that loves is your new mode of operation. Roll on!

Chapter 5

THE ROLE OF WORDS

> *"Kind words can be short and easy to speak, but their echoes are truly endless."*
>
> — MOTHER TERESA —

In Shakespeare's play, Hamlet, a prayer by Claudius the King includes the following: "My words fly up, my thoughts remain below. Words without thought to heaven never go." I saw this play in the Pantages Theater in Hollywood as a young adult with a date. Richard Harris was the star of the play at the time. I will never forget those words. Getting answers to my prayers was top of my mind at the time. These words have had an indelible print on my mind even to this day.

It seems to me that God is a God of congruence. His words actually do match his actions the same yesterday, today and forever. So with that same sincerity should we speak the words of encouragement to others close and far. There's never a need to criticize. My family was critical of each other in the household where I grew up. Following that example, I have done my fair share of criticism and it has never helped anyone love me more; come closer to me; believe in me; or do what I asked. If your thought is for correction, you can use words that do not criticize as you help that loving correction. Words like, "May I show you a way that might help you achieve what you would like to achieve?" "May I suggest a different approach?" The key here is to ask permission. If permission is not granted for your advice or help, the conversation is over for the moment. They are not open to being teachable. You can spend your time with those who are more teachable. Even if they really need to know what you know.

Permit me to illustrate a word spectrum. On the left of the spectrum are words that damage, demean, discourage, demote, show disdain, etc. On the right are words that encourage, uplift, inspire, invigorate, spark imagination, enlighten, etc. Words in the middle are subjective and can be taken one way or another. If you are operating on the right with words on the spectrum, then your character is set and people will listen to you because they know you provide encouragement for the good choices they make. It's who you are. They expect it. And because of that mindset, they will indeed listen and not think it is a criticism because that would be out of character for you. On the other hand, if your words regularly correct with sharp criticisms that make others feel small, you have built a barrier for the clear reception of your advice or correction. Your words could fall on deaf ears because people get tired of criticism and grow weary of Debbie and Donny Downer.

Growing up, I had a cassette tape recorder to capture my voice. When I played it back, it never sounded like the person who was talking in my head and out loud. I didn't like my voice because it didn't sound like me. Taking an idea or thought to words was also a challenge for me. When I realized this weakness, I decided to listen to myself more and determine if what I was saying made any sense to me. Sometimes, it didn't. I worked on making the story have a point or making what I was saying relevant to the conversational subject at the moment. Listening to your own vocabulary can have a similar effect on you. The words that we use can really brighten a day or bring on the doom and gloom. Do you know people who emit sunshine? Do you want to be with them or with Gary and Greta Gloom? Be that person you want to be with.

In competitive sports, it's fun to talk smack. But, is it fun to receive it? Well, it really depends on how it was given. For example, I play pickleball. When a person on the other team makes a shot that helps my team, I might say to them, "I love it when you choose to be on my team!" Most of the time they just laugh. They don't feel kicked to the curb, but they feel part of the WHOLE team rather than an opposing team. Yes, talking smack can be fun, especially when kind and thoughtful humor is inserted. Tennis games start with the words, Love All. I am trying to encourage my pickleball friends to start our pickleball games with Love Everyone. Only a few takers.

Using words of humor really help diffuse many tense situations. My brother was recently diagnosed with terminal cancer. I went to visit him and a niece and nephew I hadn't seen for a while were at his home. The conversation was rather lively as my brother sat in dull pain in the corner conserving energy and observing. After an hour or so of catching up, my brother became tired and got up to go take a nap. On his way out, he said, "Sorry to dominate the conversation."

He was absolutely silent the whole time. We all laughed at his sense of humor because there were many times, when he was not ill, that he definitely was the dominant force. Ironic and humorous words can create the tethers that bind us together. On a sour note, we will also remember the pain of demeaning or derogatory words. Choose carefully.

During the process of writing letters to my mother, she came across a list of great suggestions of how to be kind and encouraging to children or others. I think that even after we all left home, she was trying to improve herself. I loved her suggestions. Here are a few:

1. Great Job!
2. You nailed it!
3. How did you do that??
4. You are sure a fast learner!
5. I am so proud of the work you did today.
6. That was outstanding!!
7. I think you have figured this out!
8. That was your best time ever!
9. They call what you do being a quick study!
10. That's the right way to do that!
11. Good job remembering!
12. I couldn't have done it better myself!
13. You really broke all your previous records today!
14. That was wonderful!
15. That was first class!
16. Keep up the good work!
17. That's exactly right!
18. Terrific!
19. You are having an amazing day
20. I am happy about the work you did!
21. You make it look so easy.
22. That's quite an improvement!
23. That's the way!
24. You make it look so easy!

25. Good for you!
26. I have never seen it done better!

A little water on young and tender plants goes a long way. Positive reinforcement can become a 'light me up' moment. It's fun to give those moments and watch the fireworks show. Part of that fireworks show is also how we talk to ourselves. First thing in the morning, many people review their affirmations and goals. This is definitely a perfect time for positive self-talk to happen. Once I heard a story of a guy who got really mad at himself. He chose to give himself the silent treatment. He didn't talk to himself for a week. I think he was an accountant and, from experience, that would be devastating! Please talk nicely to yourself. You are important!

Validation is a real thing for you and me. Words can pump us up or deflate us. It really depends on our diction. Once I heard a story of a defamation suit that was being tried in court. The judge heard the case and then recessed for a day. Prior to the recess, the judge commanded the defendant to write down all the things that he thought the petitioner had done wrong on a piece of paper. All the tales of woe; all the accusations. Then, the defendant was to tear the accusations up into small pieces of paper and scatter the pieces on his way home that day. When the trial reconvened the next day, the judge asked the defendant if he had done what he had asked. The defendant confirmed. He then sentenced the defendant to pick up all the complaints and bits of paper that he had scattered the previous day. Unkind words make an imprint that sometimes cannot be retracted. Choose well how you express your thoughts through speech.

Our tongue has the opportunity to bless or curse. It's interesting how the blessings fill the cup of the one being praised and that praise is very likely passed on to others. If someone is having a good day because of what someone said, it may be likely that they will also help others have a good day. On the other hand, the person having a bad day will likewise desire everyone to be miserable like themselves. What words will you serve up today?

Chapter 6

THE ROLE OF SERVICE

> *"The fruit of love is service which is compassion in action."*
>
> — MOTHER TERESA —

Several years ago, my wife found out about a local cause that touched our hearts. She told me the story about it and I was hooked. The story is so good that I asked permission to write it below.

TAN'S TREATS

"Tan" was an amazing influence in the lives of many. He was a great son, brother, uncle, friend, and role model. When Tanner passed away in a tragic accident, we (the founders of Tan's Treats) were devastated and determined to live a life like he had. Tanner spent so much of his life helping those around him and we wanted to be able to teach our children, who didn't all get a chance to know him, about what a great example he was to all of those around him. When Tanner was in elementary school, his Mom noticed that he was coming home from school starving. When she approached him about it, she learned that he had been giving his lunch to a boy in his class that didn't have lunch. For the rest of that year, Tanner took two lunches to school, one for himself and one for his friend. What better way to continue Tanner's legacy than to make sure that all children have the food that they need every day. Our goal is to provide food on weekends and holiday breaks when school lunch programs don't provide the food needed. We started "Tan's Treats" so we could keep on giving the way that Tanner would have. We are an organization of his family and friends who are dedicated to serving those around us as he would have done and are determined to make sure there are no hungry kids in our community.

To donate to this cause, visit: http://tanstreats.com/.

Every community has opportunities galore to serve. What do you like to do? If you are not averse to blood, you might consider giving blood to your local Red Cross. They keep track of how often and how much blood you give and if you ever need blood, you will be so very glad you gave. The political system also is in need of volunteers, especially at election time. Domestically, you could fix dinner or even run the vacuum cleaner.

There are opportunities to feed the homeless at soup kitchens. Close to me is a church that has a meal for anyone to come and enjoy at 5 pm every day. Volunteers cook the dinner and serve it with a smile. The community donates the food and other churches in the community donate either food or volunteers from their congregation. It's a great system that has worked for years. In addition, the city has researched the top ten homeless shelters in the country and have taken the best ideas from them all to create our own. There are sleeping quarters. There's a play area. There's a kitchen. There's a thrift store. There are opportunities for work and service in the shelter for the residents. And, there is a police substation on site. It's safe. It's well run.

CHAPTER 6: THE ROLE OF SERVICE

And volunteers make dinner for the grateful residents every day. It's so satisfying for both the giver and recipient.

From a business standpoint, I thought it would be useful to serve on a board of directors at a local chamber of commerce. It was a voluntary, non-paid position. As I reflect, my motives were not so much about service as it was about self-promotion. My hopes were for business contacts to be able to further my own business. I haven't received a single client from this association. The only benefit for me was the love gained for the other board members and the chamber office manager. When did my motive filled desires refine to do the service, just because? For me, it was when I decided to provide service to the chamber without regard for outcome. With this new heart of service, I was able to put together a visitor guide that became the most popular visitor guide to date. To me it was a work of love and it seemed to be received as such. When the service was sent out with pure motives of love, it was received as such. It became non-transactional. The manifestation was love for the community where I was serving. And, thankfully it was received as such.

So, let's talk about this mindset of love by doing service. The change for me with the chamber of commerce was when it moved from selfish to selfless. When that happened, and my motives were purely out of love, the dynamics and joy of the service came to me. Before that, it was frustrating. I was wondering what I was doing spending all this time working so hard on a visitor guide. For what? Then I saw the value of getting to know the members and what they do. I saw a great opportunity to learn what others were doing to make the community a better place to live. I saw others with pure motives to serve without recompense because it was the right thing to do. I saw the successes of others in the community and applauded their making the world a better place by doing what they did best... serving the community with their services or products. Granted, the self-servers are still out there, but there are so many more that just do the right thing because it is the right thing to do. And they give freely to the community that supports them in their efforts.

There's an organization worth mentioning here that is all about service. JustServe.org is an organization that is a clearing house, so to speak, of various voluntary opportunities in the community and around the world. If a non-profit in the area has need of volunteers, they just post a listing on JustServe.org and the volunteers tell Just Serve that they are going to be there to provide the service. Service can be in person or remote. It can be event related or ongoing service on a regular basis. It can be talent based or helper based to accomplish a cause.

When the kids were home, we decided we just wanted to go see how much trash we could pick up in an hour or two. We laid some ground rules for safety and went out on a local street near our home and started walking, sticks and bags in hand. We came back with three bags full of trash for just a little time out of our day to improve the community. More importantly, I think the children were improved because they felt the value of doing service when nobody assigned it, nobody was watching, and it seemed like a thankless job. They quietly made what was in their reach better. There's a neighbor who every two weeks quietly goes up and down the street picking up trash. Be that good neighbor.

A word needs to be mentioned about church service. It has been done for hundreds of years. The early Christian missionaries came to the Americas to spread the love of God and Christ with the idea of helping others see the better things of life. Missionary opportunities still abound in many churches. Volunteering to teach, do activities for children, speak, sing, preach or just be a good example of a disciple of Jesus Christ are great places to serve. The whole idea of doing something without compensation, for someone you have never met, without expecting any thanks is the epitome of loving service. This type of service is definitely true brotherly love in action.

The Great Salt Lake and the Dead Sea have something in common. They both have water going in but they both don't have an outlet. Love needs an outlet. Love needs to be sent forth. Service is a great way to send it out without any expectation of it ever coming back your way. Consider the widows who cannot pay to have their lawns mowed. Or the ragged children who make their own play and scrap for their own food. They may be dirty and unkempt, but they still are in a position to be cared for and taught to love, regardless of the circumstance. Are you perhaps waiting for time? Are you possibly too busy to care? Take a pause and look around. Your regrets at the end of your life will most likely not be that you didn't spend enough time at the office. It will be that you didn't help enough or help someone you knew needed help or chose not to love. Serving is help. Serving is love.

There may not be horns trumpeting or accolades galore and you may not change the world. But each of us can do what is within our reach. We can lift where we stand in our communities, our schools, and our churches. All service opportunities are not created equal. Some require a lot of time. Some very little for great results. Some might be a solitary task and others can be very social and vibrant. I am confident that for every personality out there, there's a service opportunity that would meet your needs.

Chapter 7

THE ROLE OF TOUCH

> *"I've learned that every day you should reach out and touch someone. People love a warm hug, or just a friendly pat on the back."*
>
> — MAYA ANGLEOU —

Early in the development of the Role of Love die, I needed some testing and proving of the theory. The theory of taking two seconds out of your day and having it change the whole course of the day was rather radical, even for me. It was the idea that a tiny investment could bring big returns. I thought it could happen if someone would actually do it. It worked for me, but would it work for others? I wanted families to test it so I supplied a die to a family with five children and I asked them to test the concept over a thirty-day period of time. The results were astonishing!

Keep in mind, the die is all about rolling it daily and GIVING that style of love away, all day that day. For this family, it was a morning choice that set the standard of conduct for the day. Instead of the "me, me, me" flavor kids can bring to family dynamics, all of a sudden it became "you, you, you." What can I do for you? In what way can I spend time with you today? What small gift might light up your day? What thoughtful words can I say to you today? Can I give you a hug? Upon follow-up, I found out that each child rolled the die individually rather than as a family. So, one day when it came time for four-year-old Jonathan to do his roll, he got very excited. "Touch! Yes!" (coupled with a fist pump). Suddenly, he went over and started beating up on his older brothers. Jonathan, being the youngest, must have somehow thought this was the way love by touch was transmitted, possibly by experiencing it himself. After trying to suppress the laughter, the mother saw this as a teaching moment for appropriate loving touch. The door was now open for teaching correct principles that could change a generation. Appropriate, soft, and loving touch.

The habit of focusing on loving every day created great results for this family. And it can for yours. One of the funny things about this die is that it was created while I was single. Because I was single, I had to look for opportunities with everyone who crossed my path. I really didn't have a significant other to practice with. The eye opener for me was that the words inspired by tennis, "love everyone," as I suggested for opening a pickleball match, kept coming back to me.

Attempts to find something good to notice about everyone is challenging sometimes and really fun! I found it works for singles and families. All you have to do is to have contact with anyone and watch for any opportunity to love in the way you rolled that day. Each day is likely to be a different style of love to express, allowing variety for ways to love.

When the Democratic candidate for president won the Iowa Primary in 2008, he made a now famous fist bump to his wife. It was an innovative way to show affection and approval. Football players do it with the body bump while jumping in the air to show approval of a well-executed play. During the Covid 19 pandemic, nobody wanted to shake hands. Elbow bumps and

CHAPTER 7: THE ROLE OF TOUCH

fist bumps or shoulder bumps were common where I live. Or, sadly nothing. No hugs, no touching of any kind. This was an introvert's dream to have such a pandemic. At the same time, it starved those who need the touch as part of their daily diet of affection.

My granddaughters have been taught to High Five. Their father made a game of it and it ends with a tease. High five; to the side; to the other side; down low (at which time they move their hand out of the way) and say Too Slow! It makes them giggle and light up when they make me miss down low. A harmless game that sends loving signals of touch. It endears me to them and them to me.

And maybe that is the test of the touch style of loving. Does the touch repel them or will it endear them to you? Touch in the wrong places can get you in some hot water with the law as well as with the person touched. Just say no to wanting to receive Karate Chops or well-placed kicks and you will keep it clean. Pats on the back (above the waist is the back…) for encouragement are perfect for those that have accomplished something worthy of patting on the back. Sometimes, this pat on the back is also coupled with words that complement the action, thought, or words expressed. Sometimes it is just a quiet acknowledgment of the words, "Well done."

Don't you love creative people who make complicated handshakes that are unique to them? It's a special bond between only those two. You may feel the envy creep up a bit that you aren't involved in the greeting or departing gestures, but use that emotion to create one for yourself and another. Love in this style can take time to develop, but that is what this exercise is all about. Think about touching appropriately. How can you touch so that others will be more encouraged to continue to do good things?

Recently, I had a brother who passed away. At the viewing, I held his cold hand for a moment. For me to properly grieve, I needed that touch. A final touch. The funeral was also full of people to hug and to help through their own grief. This whole concept of touch is to share the burdens of one another and to lift each other. Whispering sweet somethings into the ears of those we touch is an added sweetness that can prolong the embrace and mark it for remembrance. It seems to me that longer hugs are remembered longer.

Some of the most endearing moments of any relationship is to wipe away the tears of another. The soft touch to the face of another seems to transmit the feelings of understanding, without the words even being said. Leaving the hand on the cheek as you do so will also pronounce a lasting effect on the receiver of your thoughtfulness and kindness. You will be remembered for your kindness, understanding, and soft touch.

One time, I was showcasing the die at a networking meeting. An injury attorney approached me with curiosity. He looked at the die, rolling it around in his fingers and said, "I want one that only has the touch symbol on all six sides." Any idea as to what was his preferred love style?

Normally, it would seem this would be a comment of what he would like to receive, but in this case, I think it was both for giving and receiving.

So is there a way to innocuously signal to another that you want a hug? My brother incorporated a great way to greet his grandchildren and children by throwing both arms high in the air when he first saw them calling out their name. In this way, it invited others to know he wanted physical contact and he was ready. He made it easy to walk into his arms and give or receive the hug.

CHAPTER 7: THE ROLE OF TOUCH

Some body language is easily read and the message properly transmitted. But how do you relay to someone you want a kiss? Maybe blow one to them earlier? Maybe start at the cheek? Maybe send them the fishy lips in a text so that meeting in person you have warmed them up? Sometimes it is just the kindness that leads up to the sweet thank you of a kiss. A kiss is also used as a greeting in many cultures. I love importing that culture wherever I go...

Kissing could be the start of soul level touch and lead to other acts of touching. Beware of starting! Sometimes, you may not want to stop. It definitely is a way to express affection by touch. Even a soft finger over the lips of the person you intend to kiss is a great way to start your momentum. It's a great warm up for those wishing to have intimacy (into-me-I-see) sometime in the next little while. Warm up is essential for getting those feelings to the point where all are satisfied. Just remember the rule of love and it will be a very pleasant experience. CARDINAL RULE: It's not about you. Look out for her/him always and you will not be disappointed, unless your partner possibly thinks love is a selfish thing. Heaven forbid you have chosen someone like that. If perhaps that is your circumstance, please don't despair. Use these stories and conversations to help them come around to know that love giving is where the joy is. It's the only direction we have control over.

Using this cardinal rule with pets is easy. They give back more than you could ever give to them. Notice that they do it in several ways. A wagging tail, a brush up against your body, a nuzzle with their head and nose, etc. Pets are definitely love multipliers. With a little investment on our part to touch them, they give so much in return. I LOVE investments like that!

The die and using it daily has helped me understand that giving is where there is hope. The more we give, the more we receive. And then our capacity to give increases so that we can send out more. This process can fill our lives with the elusive joy and happiness others only dream about. This is your time. This is your day to lay your claim to the love that can come to you unabated. No holds barred.

Chapter 8

THE ROLE OF GIFTS

"Love never asks, it always gives."

— GANDHI —

Tyler rolled Gifts one day. He knew his wife didn't particularly respond to gifts, so he became creative. His wife loved hearing the words of love. That was her preferred style of love to receive. So, he wrote her a note and wrapped it up as a gift. She absolutely loved his creativity and the care he took to practice love that day.

This choice of loving every day requires some creativity. Gifts is one of those categories that could envelope all the other types of love by simply packaging. For example, if you rolled Time, how could you see yourself giving that as a gift? Spending time with an elderly person at a retirement center would brighten their day, and yours. It especially could be counted as a gift if you were even more specific and found someone at the retirement center who was having a birthday. Make the day special for them. Most centers celebrate the birthdays for the month on one special day, but the specific day for the person may pass without fanfare. Your gift could be to change that. Brightening the day of one person at a time is something we can do. We do what is within our reach and hope others will do the same.

Thoughtful gift giving has been an art that I have had to

acquire. My family was very poor growing up and it was a challenge. One time, after I had moved out, my mother sent me a gift that was packaged in a room filter box for smokers. She and my father both smoked. My thoughts were, huh? I don't even smoke. And I wasn't hanging around people that smoked. It didn't make any sense to me, except that I had in the past received disjointed gifts from her. In many instances, I realized it may have been all she had to give. When a person gives you a gift, there is this feeling of obligation that you must keep the gift. At least for me. I somehow didn't feel that way with this room filter for smoking. I took it back to a department store, received full credit and traded that credit for a winter coat that I needed. A couple of months later, I received a call from the store that a customer had purchased my return and opened it up and there was homemade fudge and candy for Christmas in the box. I laughed hysterically at what I had done with my mother's famous Christmas fudge. The department store requested I send the funds for the coat, which I did.

From that time, I have learned to listen to people around me on what they might like or need. I knew how it felt to get a gift that had my head shaking. So, I started to make mental and physical notes and present the gifts at the appropriate times. They are usually so surprised that I would give them something they wanted and wonder how I knew. Clues are given every day. My wife used to say she hated her blender. Note to self. The next holiday, guess what was the gift? It doesn't take a master at memorization to make notes for the needs and wants of another.

Rather, it is the thoughtful doing that endears others when the gifts are appropriate. Delivery of love and remembering to love are gifts all by themselves. If you can master this, you will do well in this style of love.

CHAPTER 8: THE ROLE OF GIFTS

This category of Gifts also can incorporate any or all of the other styles of love. Take Service for example. The gift of Service can change a stressful situation to a situation of manageability. Service organizations like the Red Cross, Doctors without Borders, Catholic Charities, etc. realize this and provide relief from the stress of disaster all the time. But that is usually over there somewhere, out of sight, or in the distance. What about service as a gift right in your own neighborhood? Not too long ago, a neighbor's husband died at age 55. They had a daughter with her two children living with them and I heard that the weeds were getting a bit out of hand. I quietly went and weeded for a couple of hours and called in some other helpers as a tag team effort to assist this new widow. It was a gift and there wasn't any knocking on the door or announcements.

One of my most favorite gifts of all time was from my wife. She had listened, watched, and written down things she loved about me for several days and typed them all up. Then, she painstakingly cut them into tiny strips and put them in a jar. There were 365 of them the first time she did it! I have saved them all and reviewing them strengthens our relationship. I love her dearly, because of how she loves me. Others will also love you dearly for how you love them. Gifts brighten the day, no matter what form they may appear, especially if they are thoughtful and pertinent.

So, where do all these gifts come from? Who has a budget to give gifts on a regular basis? It can be a challenge if you think of it in those terms. Frankly, we all have gifts or talents we are given and we have the opportunities to learn what they are and use them to bless our life and the lives of others. Lots of gifts are natural, but other gifts are developed. Like playing the piano, sports, writing, reading, telling a story, laughing, organizing, shopping, singing, or just plain listening. All those could be gifts given on days the die suggests you watch for opportunities to give. My son just rolls the die again when he rolls Gifts because he can't think of anything immediately. I laugh with him when the gift icon comes up again on the second roll.

One of the most gratifying things about rolling the die for me has been the opportunity to recognize the gifts of others. The recognition of them might be a gift of validation. Twice in the last week when I went to visit my son on the east coast, people around me said they felt validated by something I noticed. Frankly, no one had ever said that to me before and I felt it a milestone of personal progress. I was actually the one being validated for the observations of others. I have been trying to validate others all this time I have rolled the die. Do you see that? The sending out of kindness came right back to me immediately. Most of the time it is not that swift, but it will come.

Each word of kindness is a gift. Every compliment to another, in sincerity, is a gift. The thoughtfulness behind your words is a gift. Sometimes, it is very unexpected and the words actually can turn to blubbering. Have you ever made someone cry for being happy? It's definitely more enjoyable than making someone cry for any other reason. In those tender moments, sometimes just the quiet closeness is enough to soothe.

Flowers make great gifts. There are also a lot of chocolate lovers out there. Plants last much longer than flowers and sometimes are an enduring choice for longer reminders of your kindness. Personally, I like gifts where I can reclaim the feelings of kindness long after the gift was given. Just my preference of a gift. Love is like that… it remains long after the shiny event, gift or compliment has worn off. Bling, bling or jewelry can have that longevity as well. For physical gifts, it's been a great activity

CHAPTER 8: THE ROLE OF GIFTS

to make a treasure hunt. It's got all the elements of the words with directions as to how to get to the next clue or prize. The anticipation of what's next is such a fun and spontaneous exercise. Mix it up, spice it up and love it up!

Isn't love itself a gift? The idea that someone loves something about you and is willing to learn more. The whole idea that, despite your flaws, someone is willing to overlook them to see the core goodness of you and express it in many ways is very validating. These friends are gifts to you when they recognize your good qualities over your warts or skin tags. And you to them. It's an interdependence and mutual appreciation. As it grows and develops, we call it love and it is indeed a gift.

A few words about the family being a gift to each of us. How many times have they stood beside us? How many times have we longed for the tight family relationship and they were there? Granted, there are times when we wish we might have been adopted to another family, but by and large, families love one another. It definitely is a gift. Having a shoulder to cry on when no one else will listen. Having a place to call home. Having those life experiences that no one else knows about… the inside jokes. The quirkiness of the dynamics and the genetic imitations all make us family. To have and hold gratitude for your loved ones is a gift. Hold on tight.

Chapter 9

THE ROLE OF TIME

"If you judge people, you have no time to love them."
— MOTHER TERESA —

Remember my fishing story with Joshua? I sent him a die in the mail for him to try and this is his story of an experience he had one day:

"I had an experience this week that I would like to share. I started my day and "rolled" Time. It took a few minutes to think about what I was going to do that day, hoping to make plans to give more time to those around me. I couldn't think of a whole lot of opportunities. But the cube kept reminding me to keep looking for chances. My work meetings were packed full that day and not a whole lot of time to spend with those attending nor did I feel like they wanted to. Everyone was rushed for close. My day just kept going and going from one meeting to another with some unplanned meetings popping up. I looked at the clock and saw how behind I was on the huge list of things I needed to do. And then I heard my daughter's voice behind me say, "Dad! You need to come see this! Sandra (a neighborhood friend) caught a praying mantis!" Without looking at her I said, "Malia, I don't have t. " But I cut myself off in mid-sentence. I looked at her and felt the reminder of my commitment that day to give a little more time to those around me. I locked my computer and walked away from the list of things to do and let my little girl take my hand to show me something special to her because I wanted her to know she will always be special to me. We held a bug together and laughed and made a simple memory. Work was right where I left off and I was able to make the deadlines I had. I'm grateful for this opportunity to be more mindful every day of the decisions I make to be more considerate of others. I am a believer that as we love those around us and let others love us, we will ascend together towards Him who loved us first."

As a teen, I had the opportunity to live with my older brother for a year or so. During this time, I cherished the time he took to help me process different activities, dates, and happenings in my life. It was a spectrum check to find out what I liked or disliked and what went well or didn't go so well. Crystallizing those thoughts as a teenager seemed to give me a clear understanding of where I stood in my own eyes, having to defend or relent on positions I chose to portray. To this day, I remember learning through these talks on how to weigh pros and cons and make better decisions with the information I had, or go get more information to make a better decision. This processing wasn't taught to me before. I remember them as teaching moments for me and the kindness and enthusiasm for which he cheered my better reasoning. After I saw the benefit of those talks, I actually began to sit hopefully in the same chair each night for another round of discussion at the feet of his wisdom.

Lowell Rex is another person in my life who taught me the value of taking time. Every month, on the first Sunday of the month, he would interview his children. He would take the time to ask them questions about their life and what they would like to do. He used expert reasoning to help them clarify their goals and then, as a father, would commit his support and help in accomplishing the chosen tasks. At the end of each interview, there was a black bag that you reached your hand into and pulled out a treat. Then, there was the loving hug. The kids clamored to be first to see what the treats were for the month. I sat in this interviewee position with Lowell several times and felt his authentic and great love for me and others. Lowell, in these circumstances, helped me understand the power of choosing not to be critical. I am quite sure I was not perfect around him or his family but I did and still highly regard Lowell for his decision to find nice things about others rather than faults. His example was encouraging.

Time seems to equate with learning. If we take the time to listen, we will have a better understanding. Those who are impatient don't ever get to the point of truly understanding unless it is in a pointed and dramatic way. I would not like the car alarm to go off, the rooster to crow, or the dogs to bark every time I misunderstood something. Impatient folks have that air of knowing it all and do not need further details. From my own sad experiences, I have learned that patience is a virtue that takes time to nurture and develop.

Consider a seed. Just putting it in the ground is a great act of faith. But without nourishment, it will not grow. Yelling at it to grow faster won't really help. Why would we do that to someone we are supposed to love? Patience is one of those ways we nourish truth. It takes time to find out all sides of a story before you can have true understanding. Many times, that understanding is not meant for judgment or for your own gossip column, but it is for peace in your own heart and passing that peaceful insight to others who might grow from your thoughtful commentary.

One of the seeds I wanted to plant in my children is the love for books. On a regular basis, they would be so excited to bring home a flier from school for the latest book club orders. I participated but only on the condition that the book had to have an award or medal associated with it. We purchased some of the best books I could have imagined! We cuddled and took the time to read, laugh, and understand the story. The time spent doing that was well worth the investment. It helped them in their school work and many of them are still avid readers. One is even a school teacher. I loved that time with my children.

A few months ago, my wife asked me to go on a bike ride. For a long time I have been wanting to ride this great big hill near our city. It probably starts at 4000 feet and descends to about 2500 feet. A great drop and paved trail follows the contour of the land with ups and downs like an exciting roller coaster. She wanted to spend time with me. I was excited to ride.

Just eighteen months earlier, my wife and I were riding our bikes and I think I must have blacked out and I went down. I don't remember being down because after I went down, I woke up in the hospital with a broken back in three places, a badly sprained neck, a concussion, and abrasions on my head, shoulders, elbows, and knees. For almost a week I was in the hospital and had back surgery to insert rods and eight screws to facilitate the healing of a vertebrae that was a 'burst' break. After six months of the rods in my back, my surgeon thought I was healed enough to be able to have the hardware removed. I was amazed at the size of the 6" rods and 3" screws. My wife thought the bike may have been the problem so she had me sell the bike. I did so, but bought another for $20 at a yard sale and fixed it up. This was one of the first excursions with my new fixed up bike. I reworked the bearings and made sure everything was smooth riding. On the way down, the trail was skinny and would really only allow one person or bike each way. I thought I mentioned I would meet her at the bottom… but probably thought it and didn't say it. By the time I got to the bottom, I had my bike set aside to lock as we traveled up by car to the start point to pick up the bike carrier. My wife came about 5-10 minutes later. She was not amused. Her idea of doing the bike ride in the first place was to talk and ride side by side together. I wanted the full slope and speed of the hill. She wanted me to be more cautious. I wanted to prove that I am resilient. Back and forth, on and on, it went until she finally declared she would never ride bikes with me again. I was going too fast and putting my life at risk again of having a bike accident. Thank goodness, she has taken time to relent and allow me to rethink my approach to spending time together. It's important to her, to me, and to others to take the time to know each other. There's no question that time is a factor in building strong and lasting relationships.

There is a teacher who rolled the die and it came to rest on Words that day. She took the time to explain the Words icon to her 3rd grade class. As a class, they practiced using their kind words that day. She, as the teacher, praised them all day. Her reward? The kids would do ANYTHING for her that day. She had them in the palm of her hands and they could learn and be molded. It was one of her best days ever! It just took a few moments to explain the style of love. Time well invested.

My early mornings are filled with pickleball games, 6 days a week. Playing pickleball with the group is a 80ish year old woman who is quite good. Early in my association with this group after a slam, she would say things like, "Would you hit the ball to your mother like that?" I thought she was trying to get me to be a nicer person. Definitely a wakeup call. I thought I was nice. Last week, on a neighboring court, a gentleman said, "Hello, Mrs. Morris!" Then he proceeded to tell us how he and this teacher had together raised wonderful children. Mrs. Morris apparently had taken the time to contact each parent and when the child did something kind, they were to write a note about it and send it with the child to school. The note was then read aloud in the classroom in front of everyone with the child standing at the head of the class. After recess each day, she would ask the children, "Did anyone see anyone do anything kind at recess today?" So, all along Mrs. Morris was trying to teach me to be kind in competitive sports. That is a subject for another whole dissertation. Not today.

Make the Time to choose to love.

Part Three

Chapter 10

THE ROLE OF RECOGNITION

"Love is the bridge between you and everything."

— RUMI —

Just last Sunday I was in church and saw someone I knew and went over to their pew. I noticed my friend Kathy had a new haircut and I said, "Cute Haircut!" You would have thought I just lit up a Christmas tree. Kathy is 74 and her husband was sitting right beside her. She became all bright-eyed and blushed and was so surprised that someone noticed. Seeing how she 'lit up,' I turned to her husband and said, "Dale, don't you also think Kathy's haircut is cute?" Sheepishly, he had his head down and would not make eye contact. Apparently, he had not noticed or said anything to his own wife about her haircut.

There are a lot of Dales out there. I know. I was one of them about a dozen years ago when I was awakened to the fact that I really had no clue what kindness or love was about. It was after the time that I had done the destination dating. I was minding my own business in Phoenix and my older sister thought I was lonely, so she introduced me to her neighbor. I warned her. "If this goes bad, it's not so bad for me, but you still have to live in the same neighborhood. Are you sure you want to do this?" She laughed and said she would be fine.

I started corresponding with this woman and absolutely LOVED her writing. She was witty and happy and darling. When asked about how many times she had been married, she said, "Counting the five husbands buried in the backyard?" I was hooked. Humor, for me, is a must in a great relationship. After about six weeks of this back-and-forth email and messenger, I wanted to hear her voice. So I asked for her phone number. She was afraid of having that exploited online so she wouldn't tell me the number… even by code. After a couple of weeks of asking, one day I checked my phone after a meeting and someone from her area code called me. I returned the call only to find out that it was her son who was going to give me her phone number verbally. I laughed that it was still coming from a third party. She told me I could ask my sister for her phone number. Not my style, but at least, at last, I had the number. I immediately called and heard her voice. Her laugh was so infectious that I could not get it out of my mind. A hilarious laugh that had all the right tones in the right places. Music to my ears. Could this be the one?

From that correspondence and subsequent conversations, we started making plans to meet. I was seven hours away by car and only had weekends to visit. So, on the first visit, I left work on Friday night at five, got to her destination at midnight, and we went for a walk. Yes, it was dark and I wanted to really see her, so I would linger under the streetlights a little longer on that first walk and match the stories and voice and the laugh to this person I had just met. To me, she seemed like a winner. I kept it to myself and did these trips for a few months, leaving Friday and returning at midnight on Sunday. I was ready to explore the question… Yes, the big question. But before that, I felt I wanted big brother's approval.

CHAPTER 10: THE ROLE OF RECOGNITION

My older brother has always been held in high esteem. I valued his opinion. But when I brought this woman to his house, his wife whisked her away, within earshot, and told her, "The only emotion the Zolman family learned growing up was anger." At first, I denied it. Then it made me MAD! Oh… wait… maybe there is a problem. Wait, wasn't my anger solved through my anger management course? Residual. I thought that if this was the perception, I had an opportunity to change that perception right now. Time to go to work and refine what I had learned.

The lights came on and somebody was finally home. I started reading books about color codes and love languages and just became more confused. However, the love styles outlined in the book *The 5 Love Languages* by Gary Chapman seemed to resonate with me on a different level than what the book expressed. I didn't understand the book. To me, it seemed that the author was advocating guesswork and I was a bad guesser. Also, it seemed awkward to me to take the survey and find out a primary love language for myself. What was I supposed to do with that? Advertise? "Hello, I am Gifts! What do you have for me today?" AWKWARD. I read it five times and definitely wasn't raised that way. How could I even have a primary love language if I was raised in a home of anger? Well, I took the survey anyway. Yup, I was Physical Touch. All that whacking at home was what I thought was love… and I must have grown to like it. My thoughts were, if I catered to someone according to the love style they liked, I was manipulating the results and it lacked the qualities of what I thought of as genuine love.

The direction of love was an issue for me in these books as well. Was my primary love style the one I liked to receive or the one I liked to give away? With that in mind, it seemed like there were ten love languages and not just five. There were five for giving and five for receiving. They were different and confusing to me. After much thought, I dissected it by what I had control over and what I did not. I realized that I can react to love given to me, but the way that love came to me and the timing wasn't necessarily something for which I pulled the strings. I can send love out without regard to the reactions of others, but I found it helpful to pay attention to their reactions. I took mental notes and sometimes written notes. I thought it was so interesting when they became lit up by something that I sent out. Noted.

I could see how Service could be a way to give to the community that you love and to others. The giving of Gifts has always been an act of love in my eyes. Spending precious Time with someone is also an act of love for that person or thing. Yes, things can be loved as well. Touch and kind words can spark thoughts of goodness in the recipient. These styles are really basic to love. I felt this was a good place to start with these basic principles. But is that it?

What is love, really? The word love has many connotations in this day and age. Unfortunately, most thoughts of it lead to sex. There are many other options. But in my experience, the very best sex is preceded by acts of kindness. Remember, I have eight children. It is these acts of kindness that truly constitute what love is all about. Sex may be one result of many, but is not necessarily a by-product of the acts of kindness we will discuss here.

Who is it that sets the standard or makes the rules about love? Who decides what love is and what is not? Where are the lines? Maybe it would be easier to ask the opposite question of who decides if there is abuse or not? Ultimately, in my opinion, it is how the recipient feels.

Profound impact of someone caring, expressing nice thoughts, a thoughtful note, an act of service, a treasured gift, or a soft touch are all appropriate ways to love. These sincere acts of kindness and caring transmit good feelings to the other person and the giver should also feel this inner satisfaction. It's not the cost of the gift or act but the sincerity of the giver. Be sincere. Sometimes it is just a phone call or a text message. Words can and do make a difference.

Sometimes it might be a pat on the arm or a kind hug. Doing something nice for someone can make their day. Mow a lawn. Read a book or write a letter for an elderly person. Leave a secret gift. Wash your neighbor's car. Relieving pain or sometimes just listening is enough. Sit with someone and hear them out. Spend time with them. The key to knowing what love is, is to know how it is received. If you can detect what that person might need or want in their time of need, you will most likely do the deed that will help you succeed.

Are you detecting that love is not a solo flight? Good call. It is DOING for others. It involves other people. Can you remember any time in your life that you have spent time with, served, given a random hug, given an anonymous gift or just complimented someone? How did you feel afterwards? That feeling is only half of the love. The other half is how they felt about what you gave. However, we only have control over what we give. Give generously!

Everyone is deserving of love. It is not for reciprocal actions. It is not because of who they are. It's all about who you are or choose to be. It is because you are a loving person. Giving love away is done because of who you have become. Remember the quote from the Sound of Music: "Love in the heart wasn't put there to stay; love isn't love 'til it's given away."

And what diffuses anger? According to the movie Anger Management and Eskimos, it's saying Goosfraba several times.

The Eskimos used it to soothe an upset baby. Some use counting to ten or twenty. Is it the pause? During this time period, I was so intent on overcoming my angry background and stereotype that I created an email account with a username Pauz10. The first three letters of my first name, the first letter of my last name and ten seconds to count before reacting. It seemed serendipitous for me to learn to pause before outbursts. Time to break the chains of traditions that are not good. Time to set a new course for loving family traditions.

So, if a person comes from a background of abuse, how do they ever find love? How does love ever come to them? Certainly, if you send out anger, it's not very likely that love is going to come back unless it is from someone that is very loving and can overlook the 'billy goat gruff' in all of us. Then, if anger or any of its ugly cousins (sarcasm, digs, insults, etc.) are continued to be sent out, the relationship becomes more of a chore to the giver of love and they exit stage right. Short term relationships seem more the norm. Anger begets anger. Love begets love. The law of the harvest is alive and well.

For a couple of years, I spent time in Japan. I knew that if I was to learn the language, I had to speak it and try to speak it regularly. These styles of love for me were a foreign language. Very alien. Very different. Almost ingenuous. I knew all about ingenuous. Do as I say, not as I do was the unspoken motto in my home growing up. My parents taught me not to drink by having their weekly date at the Maverick Bar. At age seventeen, I decided that if I did anything in life, I was to work as hard as I could to make my words match my actions. I started to become very quiet… amazingly that gave me permission to do nothing! Yup, words and actions match!

The paradigm shift for me came when I started a game for myself. I created icons that represented the five basic styles of love. I put them on a die with the sixth side of the die representing "surprise me." Each day I would roll the die and that would be the style of love I would express or give out all day that day. I was watching for opportunities to love. With every person I met, I would consider the question, "How or what about that person can I love today?" I was busy watching for the good parts of people and had no time for looking for faults anymore. I was watching for opportunities to love in that specific way that I chose for the day. Marvelous things began to happen to me. I saw. I thought. I did, and people lit up.

The next day it was usually a different style to practice. Over a thirty-day period, I became familiar with the five basic styles of love. I became a love linguist or a love stylist. Not only did I understand what to give away in a loving way, but I could newly see love coming my way from others who had been consistently trying to love me. It was as if I had been thinking my sight was fine and then went to the optician and got glasses. With these new eyes I could really see! Have you ever heard a word for the first time and learned it? Then, you began to hear the word every day. Love from others is all around us, if we only learn how to recognize it by learning to give it away in various styles.

What amazed me the most is what Kathy did when I gave her a compliment. People light up when you truly connect with them in a loving way. It's visible. It's apparent. It's easy to read. Hmmmm, they liked that… is the note taking your brain is doing. Remember that style for next time. Kathy likes to hear the words. The words lit her up. And when they light up, take notes. It's not sexual. It's not forward. It's not abuse. It's genuine love and care. I used to be like Dale, unable to recognize what lights people up. I like my new eyes to see, my new ears to hear, and having a heart that understands better how to love. Paying attention can help us all become better lights and beacons to lift others. Determine to be the light.

Chapter 11

THE ROLE OF "LIGHT ME UP"

> *"Set your life on fire.
> Seek those who fan your flames."*
>
> — RUMI —

The habit of love is just like any other habit, except it is a good habit and one you will want to keep your whole life. This habit can be a North Star for you. It can be a constant in your life as chaos surrounds you at every corner. The principles of love transcend the mundane of this life and keep us remembered for generations to come, if we plant the seeds, grow the trees and nurture them well. Love is the life-spring for those who want a more fulfilled life. Love is an investment that will bring big dividends in ways you cannot imagine. For example, I remember both my grandmothers, but never knew my grandfathers because they died before I was born. One grandmother I remember in kind accolades and the other was harsh and grouchy and mean. How will you be remembered?

It's these habits of love and kind humor that can help people be their best. Some of you may remember when President Reagan was shot and in the operating room said to the doctor, "I hope you are a Republican." Great sense of humor in tense situations. The practice of these principles and styles of love will sink deep into your soul and you will have the ability to push through hard times with love instead of stress that takes you to another place.

As you focus on the virtues of others and light up their lives, it will give you lasting pleasure and confidence in large and small groups as well as individual one-to-one contact. The clouds of judgment and criticism will always be around, but you are redefining what a 'fair weather friend' really is. Instead of someone who is there when things are good for you, a friend is present and brings fair weather all the time. A friend is one who brings inspiration. You are that friend who can light up the room with your positive approach to human kind. You become the beacon that is set on the hill to shine for all to be able to see the good you see. The good you see in them.

Habits of love leave a lot of room for understanding. Love begets love. The soft tones of voice don't demean or hurt or make afraid. They draw others near rather than repel them. The musical tones of love create a symphony and chorus of compassion and empathy. They sing the songs of affection in a way that supports all the styles of love. These sweet tones also ring true to those who were raised in angry circumstances. It can lift those and encourage them to also think and enjoy the musical overtones of well thought out acts of love, as they practice and incorporate them into their lives.

The muscle memory of having kind thoughts that translate into kind actions will grow stronger as you exercise those kind options. The other than kind options will always be there, but you can make the better choice. It will transform you. It will thrill you to see those you love, even in passing, light up when you get it right. The key is to always be sending out love. That's the right thing to do. It is about you only in that regard. Otherwise, it is all about them. Your strength of that memory mus-

CHAPTER 11: THE ROLE OF "LIGHT ME UP"

cle tells you what kindness you have received and liked. As you duplicate that effort and find your own strengths in that regard, you will realize that others are definitely at different levels. You will find the 80ish year old pickleball teachers that are trying to teach you to love even more. Be better and kinder, even in a competitive sport.

There is a philosophy that says you really can't get rid of anything bad until you have chosen a replacement. This book is a philosophy of using all the good you can imagine to crowd out and choke the bad out of your system. It's a sprinkling of good that you send out that makes you so busy you cannot think of the evil a person might have. In some cases, you may have to convince someone of their goodness, contrary to their own thoughts. Regularly watering that plant will indeed crowd out the evil if it is done in small doses and with kindness. A gushing firehose could kill or seem ingenuous.

This idea of love is one that fosters unity. Hate is the opposition that breaks ties to sometimes good things. Like parents. Like church. Like principles. There are laws that seem universal as they relate to love. Love brings the best out of people. Hate has its own reputation of discord to uphold.

Through love, we can become enough. We can become our full potential as we see the potential in others. Remember, we only have control over what we send out... not what we receive. We do control how we react to what we receive, but that's it. The die helped me to deeply understand the styles of love that I sent out so that I might see them when they came back, and respond accordingly.

Love heals. This is the antithesis of the idea that prevails about fixing something by breaking it first. Why do they call it breaking a horse? Or breaking men who are incarcerated?

Freedom comes from the breaking of the chains that hold them back from being what they can be. The idea that you can love someone into change for the better is definitely not a reason to marry them. This desire to change comes from within each of us. The hall monitor is yourself. I am not responsible for your change. Neither is my spouse responsible for mine. Change is an individual responsibility. The dogged determination to be better has to become stronger than the SOS(same old stuff), different day. The desire to choose to love and have that choice fill your heart and mind is the secret sauce to transformation. The cheerleaders for you are the ones you touch. They are the ones you reach out to and heal with your acts of kindness. They are the ones who heal you, without ever knowing that is what they are doing. Their responses to your kindness are what inspire you to continue the process of becoming. The healing comes only after you have given the healing balm yourself.

As you sharpen your observation skills, you are sharpening your ability to love. Observe what lights people up. Observe the effect your vocabulary might have on another. Study your thoughts to actions. Work on the idea that congruence of thought and action defines harmony. Someone has aptly said that there isn't a challenge more daunting than the challenge of improving yourself. Again, I say, it's not about you. If you remember that, you will focus on the happiness of others and that is where you will find YOUR change. That is where you will find your happiness. Therein lies your own healing.

There will be the opposite of love out there as long as we choose to focus on the me, me, me of the world. When selfishness prevails, so will anger. When selflessness prevails, so will love. It will be how we treat others. It will be the crowning moments of our life. What will be written in our obituary is how love prevailed in our lives. How we chose to give love in response to evil and not evil for evil. The trends about fairness would say giving evil for evil is fair. The reality is that it spreads more evil. John Donne was right in his prose, "No man is an Island." A little bit of kindness starts with you. Do it. Do it now.

Love doesn't go away… we just forget about it in our busy lives. The clamor of the hour makes more noise than the still and quiet acts of kindness and love. We pay more attention to the squeaky wheels of life than the quiet tones of sweetness. The crying baby gets taken out so that others can enjoy the ballads of love. Yet, even the crying baby is trying to learn to communicate love by expressing themselves. There's a baby like that in all of us wanting, hoping, and yearning for the kindness of another. Be the one to give that away. I guarantee it will come back some day just in the nick of time when you need it. Keep the constant of love in your life and it will keep you! Make it your choice.

AN INVITATION

I hope you enjoyed this book and that it helps you define ways to love more consistently.

If you would like to join a community of love fueled people who are working to improve the amount of love they experience daily, please join us in any of my Social Media groups listed below. You will be welcomed by like-minded people who are interested in making the world a better place, starting with themselves.

Feel free to ask me or the community anything about the subject of love. We also invite you to submit your own transformation story, if you feel inspired.

Way to connect:

- https://www.linkedin.com/company/roleoflovedice

- https://www.youtube.com/channel/UC1kniwkoHIW9EA5Ojv7NuLA

- https://tiktok.com/@roleoflovedice

- https://facebook.com/roleoflovedice

- https://instagram.com/roleoflovedice/

- https://pinterest.com/roleoflovedice

- https://twitter.com/roleoflovedice

Feedback Welcome.

I invite you to tell me what resonated with you as you read this book.

What have you learned about love? Which love style is easy for you to practice? And which ones are a challenge? I will personally respond to your email:

lovesrole@gmail.com

Love, Paul

ABOUT THE AUTHOR

Growing up in a family of abuse, physical touch became Paul Zolman's preferred love style. It was the only thing that he could count on regularly with any consistency. He started to think this was the only way to express love. But deep inside, he knew this was a twisted belief. He wanted a better life for himself and a better way of expressing and receiving love, so he created the Role of Love dice and the process he describes in this book.

The Role of Love helped him grow beyond his childhood of abuse to become a person who can find the good in anyone in any circumstance. He is now able to express love in a positive way toward anyone he meets. This truly is the Role of Love.

Join Paul in your own journey; visit roleoflovedice.com.

www.ingramcontent.com/pod-product-compliance
Lightning Source LLC
Chambersburg PA
CBHW070203100426
42743CB00013B/3034